BONE OF MY BONE

BONE OF MY BONE

JOANNA HENTON

CONTENTS

1	1	1
2	2	3
3	3	4
4	4	5
5	5	6
6	6	7
7	7	9
8	8	12
9	9	14
10	10	15
11	11	17
12	12	22
13	13	24
14	14	30
15	15	31
16	16	39
17	17	40
18	18	47
19	19	48

| IV | –

20 | 20 55
21 | 21 60
22 | 22 61
23 | 23 62

BONE OF MY BONE
JoAnna Henton

|2| -

2

Copyright © 2024 JoAnna Henton
All rights reserved.

No part of this publication may be reproduced, distributed, or transmitted in any form or by any means, including photocopying, recording, or other electronic or mechanical methods, without the prior written permission of the publisher, except in the case of brief quotations embodied in critical reviews and certain other noncommercial uses permitted by copyright law. For permission requests, contact the publisher at the address below.

JoAnna Henton
10401 Brockington Road, Ste 1032
Sherwood, Arkansas 72120
Phone: 501-297-3385

Scripture quotations, unless otherwise noted, are taken from the Holy Bible and are used with permission.

Printed in the United States of America.

Second Edition

4

TABLE OF CONTENTS

Preface 14

Chapter 1
The Anatomy of Connection 18

Chapter
My Other Self 27

Chapter 3
Imbalance 39

Chapter 4
The Road to Recovery 50

Chapter 5
Journey's End 60

Chapter 6
Bone of My Bone 70

Special acknowledgment

This book is dedicated to the memory of my mom, Brenda Henton Lognion, whose unwavering strength and grace under fire remained an enduring inspiration. Rest in Him.

Sunrise 08/17/1953 – **Sunset** 12/12/2022

FOREWORD

Life is an intricate tapestry, each thread interwoven with moments of joy, struggle, and profound self-discovery. Like the fragile yet unyielding framework of our bones, we are held together by connections—some strong and enduring, others weakened or fractured by the weight of time and circumstance. As the psalmist declares, *"You knit me together in my mother's womb" (Psalm 139:13)*, so too does each experience shape and bind us into a mosaic of divine intention and purpose.

In *Bone of My Bone*, my daughter JoAnna invite you to examine the very foundation of our existence—the connections that nurture life and the disconnections that hinder it. She draws a striking parallel between our spiritual and emotional lives and the human body, where even the smallest fracture can disrupt the entire system. Yet, as the Scriptures remind us, even brokenness carries the promise of restoration.

When Ezekiel stood in the valley of dry bones, he witnessed God's breath revive what seemed lost forever (Ezekiel 37). This powerful image of renewal serves as a guiding theme throughout this work: no matter how fragmented our lives may seem, there is always hope for wholeness.

Through a narrative steeped in honesty and vulnerability, JoAnna takes us on a journey of reflection and healing. Each chapter explores the delicate balance between the heart, swayed by emotion, and the mind, rooted in logic. Without harmony between these two, the soul becomes unsettled, and the path forward feels unclear. Yet, the author shows us that this balance is attainable—not through sheer willpower but by submitting to the divine orchestration of the Creator.

This book is more than a mirror reflecting our inner turmoil; it is a call to action.

It challenges us to confront the cracks in our lives, the places where connection has faltered, and to embrace the process of restoration.

Like the mending of a broken bone, recovery is not instantaneous. It requires patience, intentionality, and faith that God is working all things together for our good (Romans 8:28). Each step, though difficult, is a reminder that healing is a journey—a daily decision to move forward, trusting that what lies ahead is greater than what was left behind.

The beauty of *Bone of My Bone* lies in its universality. The struggles, doubts, and longings shared within these pages resonate deeply because they echo the cry of every soul seeking wholeness.

We are reminded that we are not alone, that our fractures are not unique but shared, and that the same God who formed us has the power to heal us. As you delve into the pages of this book,

may you find the courage to face the imbalances in your life, the hope to believe in renewal, and the faith to trust the process.

Let this book be a guide, a light on your path, and a balm for your soul. Remember that the cracks in your foundation do not define you—they prepare you for the extraordinary purpose God has for your life.

In the hands of the Master Potter, even the most shattered clay can be molded into something beautiful. You are fearfully and wonderfully made, and the journey you are about to embark on will remind you of the truth that has always been within: healing, connection, and wholeness are possible promises.

Many seek peace but find themselves battling internal chaos. They want to be a light to others, but the unchecked anger, bitterness, or sorrow they carry dims that light.

These hindrances don't just affect your personal walk with God; they also limit your ability to reflect His love and draw others closer to Him. After all, how can you minister hope when your own heart is entangled in despair? How can you offer the light of truth when shadows of doubt cloud your own perspective?

This book serves as a guide to confront those very hindrances, offering not just a path to personal healing but a blueprint for living a life of alignment, purpose, and connection with God. Through its pages, you'll be challenged to address the cracks in your foundation, rediscover the strength and resilience God has placed within you, and step into the fullness of His calling.

As you embark on this journey, prepare to be stretched, inspired, and renewed. Expect to see your relationship with God deepen and your ability to minister to others strengthened. For when your heart is free and your spirit aligned with the Source, you become a and you flow—unhindered and abundant.

"Affectionally known as Daddy"
Apostle Alfred Henton

Preface

This book is more than a collection of reflections; it is a journey—a personal exploration of healing, growth, and transformation. At its core, it is a story of finding clarity amidst chaos, strength in weakness, and purpose in pain. We all encounter cracks in our lives—moments when the foundation we've built feels unstable, when the connection between our heart and mind feels broken, and when the weight of life's challenges threatens to overwhelm us. These cracks may appear small at first, but left unattended, they grow, leaving us searching for answers, for healing, and for hope.

This book was born out of my own journey to repair those cracks. It's a testimony to the power of self-awareness, faith, and persistence. Through the process of reflection, I discovered that healing doesn't come from ignoring the pain or rushing through the process.

It comes from confronting the issues head-on, learning from them, and allowing God to work in the broken places.

Whether you are dealing with unresolved hurts, navigating emotional chaos, or simply seeking a deeper connection with yourself and with God, this book is an invitation to walk alongside me on this path to wholeness. It's a reminder that you are not alone and that no matter how broken you feel, there is always a way forward.

I invite you to take this journey with an open heart and mind. My prayer is that these words encourage you, challenge you, and inspire you to take the first step toward your own healing. You are not beyond repair. You are not too far gone. And with every decision you make to move forward, you are stepping into the fullness of who you were created to be.

Let this be the beginning of your journey to healing, hope, and abundant life.

9

10

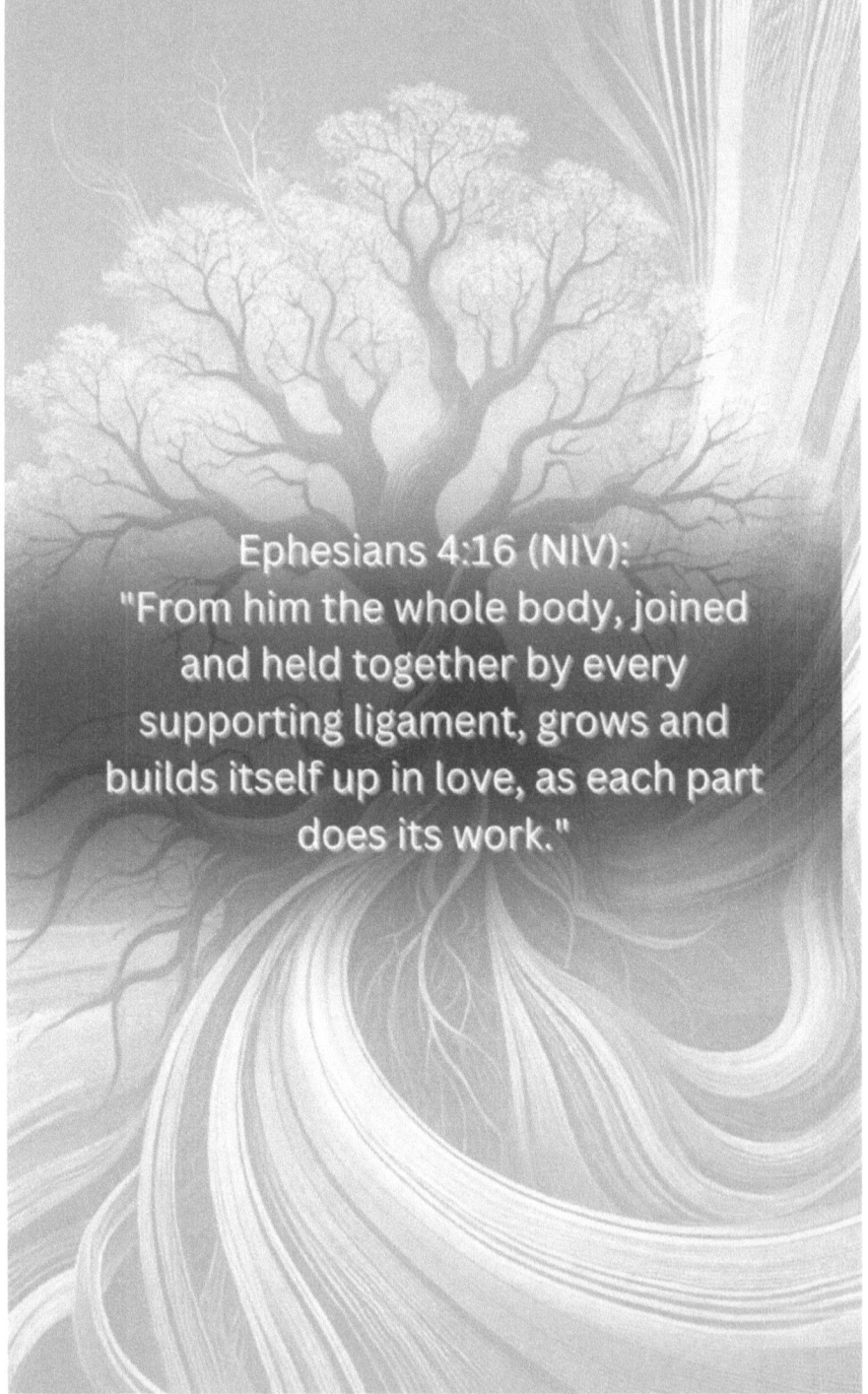

Chapter 1: The Anatomy of Connection

The word *bone* carries a profound weight. It's more than a structural element of the body; it signifies connection, strength, and unity. Bones are designed
to fit together, to create a framework that supports life. Yet, when a crack appears, even the smallest fracture, the entire system responds, signaling something is amiss. Pain becomes the body's messenger, an unrelenting voice demanding attention. The more we ignore it, the greater the damage grows, spiraling into dysfunction.

Have you ever felt the urgent pull to address something, only to shove it aside, hoping it would resolve itself?

Perhaps it was a relationship on the brink, a decision that demanded clarity, or a moment where truth pressed against your soul.

You knew the signs were there—little nudges from within, whispers from the Spirit—but you dismissed them. Over time, those gentle signals transformed into unyielding reminders, evidence of unresolved matters.

The Power of Connection

Connection isn't just a concept; it's a necessity. True connection brings peace, harmony, and alignment—not just with others, but within ourselves and with God. When we connect with the *Source*, life flows. The Source is the heartbeat of our existence: our dreams, motivations, and God-given purpose. But when disconnection creeps in, everything feels chaotic.

Think of the moments when life feels like a whirlwind, tossing you in every direction.

Your footing feels unsteady, your focus splinters, and confusion reigns. You grasp at fragments, desperately seeking the way back. But what happens when the way back feels lost? When the connection feels severed beyond repair? What then?

The answer lies in the *process*—the process of reconnection. It's a journey, and its length depends on how willingly we take responsibility for the cracks in our system. Acknowledging the fractures is the first step toward healing.

Though it may seem daunting, every broken piece holds potential. Rebuilding from shattered places can yield something even more beautiful than before.

Small Cracks, Big Consequences

Isn't it remarkable how a small crack can cause so much damage? At first, it's barely noticeable—a minor inconvenience, a fleeting discomfort. But left unattended, it grows.

Before you know it, the weight of neglect compounds, and uneasiness takes root. What started as a slight misalignment now feels like an insurmountable chasm.

For me, the cracks often appeared when I was at my most eager, ready to embark on new journeys. I would dream big, plan meticulously, and envision success. But then, somewhere between the dreaming and the doing, doubt would creep in. My heart, weighed down by fear, would lag behind my mind's readiness. The war within began—a battle between my bold aspirations and the insecurities lurking beneath the surface.

The Battle Within

"How did I get here?" I've asked myself that question more times than I can count. Lost in a maze of expectations, others and my own I often wondered if anyone truly knew me. Worse, I wasn't sure I knew myself anymore. The questions were endless: *Who am I? Where did I go? How long have I been lost?*

It's tempting to look outward for answers, to let others dictate our identity. But here's the truth: when we view ourselves through the lens of others' opinions, we lose sight of who God created us to be. Our assignment is uniquely ours, crafted by the Creator. And if we lose focus on that truth, we risk permanent disconnection from our purpose.

Reconnection: A Divine Invitation

Reconnection isn't just about finding your way back; it's about discovering something greater. It's about aligning with God, the ultimate Source of strength and purpose. The process isn't easy—it demands introspection, humility, and a willingness to confront the cracks. But the reward is immense.

No matter how broken, scattered, or shattered you feel, restoration is always possible. In God's hands, the pieces of your life can be made whole again.

Like a bone healing after a fracture, the process may take time,

but the result is stronger, more resilient, and more beautiful than before.

The journey of reconnection begins with a single decision: to stop ignoring the pain and start seeking the Source. It's in that decision that healing begins, and it's through that healing that we come to understand the true meaning of being "bone of my bone." Not just in scripture, but in every moment of our lives.

It's one thing to recognize the crack in the system; it's another to acknowledge its impact on every aspect of your life.

Cracks don't just weaken the structure—they disrupt the flow.

Whether it's the flow of blood in the body or the flow of purpose in life, the disruption is a signal, a call to action.

Ignoring it doesn't make it disappear; it only allows it to fester and grow, silently undermining the foundation.

Bones don't exist in isolation. They are part of a complex system that relies on connection and alignment to function properly. In the same way, our lives require alignment—alignment with purpose, with others, and most importantly, with God.

When we lose this alignment, we feel it in our spirit, often manifesting as anxiety, frustration, or a sense of being lost.

Disconnection doesn't always announce itself with a loud crash. Sometimes, it's a quiet drift—a gradual pulling away that's almost imperceptible. You may start to feel it as a subtle discomfort, a nagging feeling that something isn't quite right. Over time, that small crack becomes a gulf, and the longer it's left unattended, the harder it becomes to bridge. But here's the beautiful truth: even in the deepest disconnection, there's hope for restoration. The body, when injured, naturally seeks to heal itself. Similarly, the spirit is drawn toward reconciliation and repair. This is the essence of grace—a divine invitation to reconnect with the Source.

No matter how far we've wandered or how fractured we've become, God's grace makes a way.

Healing, however, requires intentionality. It's not enough to hope the crack will mend on its own.

Healing demands that we stop, assess, and take responsibility for what's broken. This is where vulnerability comes in. Acknowledging the break means admitting we need help—sometimes from others, always from God. It's in this humility that the process of restoration begins. What's remarkable about bones is that when they heal, they often become stronger at the point of the fracture. The same is true for us.

When we face our brokenness and allow God to work in us, the areas where we were once weak become our greatest strengths. But we must be willing to embrace the process, no matter how painful or challenging it might be. Reconnection isn't just about fixing what's broken; it's about rediscovering what was always there.

It's about remembering who we are—children of God, fearfully and wonderfully made. It's about reclaiming the dreams and passions that disconnection tried to steal. And most importantly, it's about realigning ourselves with the One who created us, the ultimate

Source of life and purpose.

When we understand this, the process of reconnection becomes less about the pain and more about the promise.

Yes, there will be discomfort, and yes, it will require effort.

But the result—a life fully aligned with God and with our purpose—is worth every step of the journey.

So, as you reflect on the cracks in your own system, know this: healing is not only possible; it's promised. With God, broken things don't just get repaired—they get transformed. And in that transformation, you'll find a strength you never knew you had, a strength rooted in connection, purpose, and grace.

12

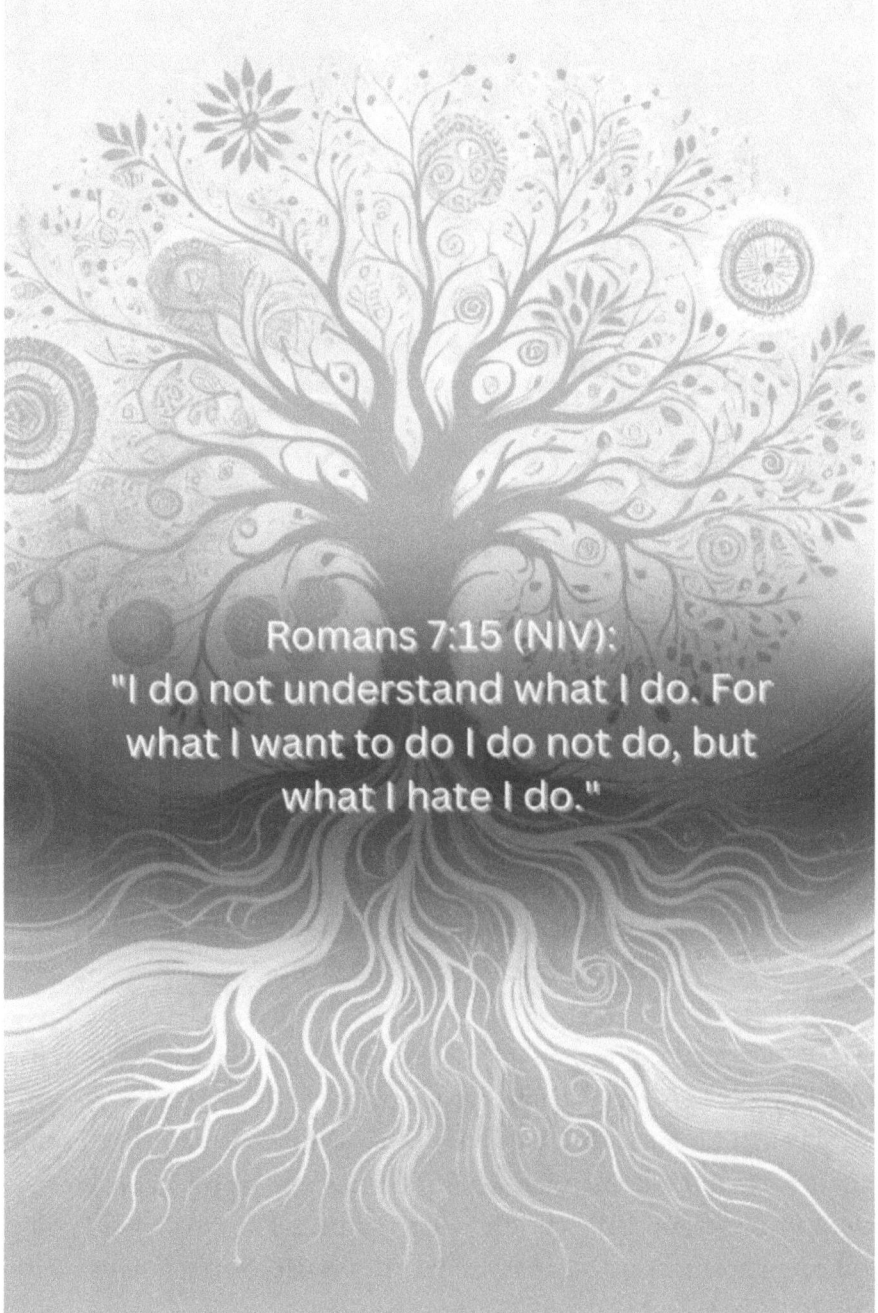

Chapter 2: My Other Self

Bone of my bone—a phrase rich with significance and depth. It evokes a sense of unity, identity, and divine craftsmanship. It's not merely about physical connection but a spiritual bond that transcends the tangible. My other self is not just a reflection of me; it is the part of me that embodies strength, courage, and purpose when I falter. It is the person God created me to be, unbound by the fears and insecurities that often hold me captive.

We were crafted by the same hands, formed with the same purpose, and fitly joined together by divine design.

There is no *me* without *you*. My other self has a confidence I sometimes lack—a boldness that sees no barriers, no opposition. It walks with assurance, unshaken by life's uncertainties. The possibilities for my other self are endless. This part of me dreams without fear, moves without hesitation, and trusts without reservation.

The War Within

Yet, there's a constant tension—a war between who I am and who I'm called to be. It's a battle between fear and faith, between security and freedom. Fear is a thief. It clogs the arteries of the heart, halting the flow of life. It fills the storage spaces of the mind with past failures, disappointments, and wounds that I've carried for far too long.

When fear takes hold, it's like a dam blocking the river of hope. The heart grows weary, and the mind becomes clouded. Instead of seeking release, we build walls—defensive mechanisms to protect what we believe is sacred.

We shut ourselves off, guarding our hearts so tightly that nothing new can enter, and nothing old can leave. But in doing so, we create stagnation. Without flow, the heart becomes burdened, and the soul begins to decay.

The Sacred Place

The sacred place within us—the core of our being—is meant to remain open, connected to the Source. My other self knows this. It draws its strength from that connection, relying on God for guidance, wisdom, and restoration. But when fear dominates, decisions become clouded, and clarity is lost.

In moments of emotional chaos, it's tempting to react impulsively, letting emotions drive our choices. But my other self knows the importance of pausing, of stepping back to evaluate. When I allow my emotions to take over—when my heart runs unchecked—I lose control. My reactions become erratic, my words harmful, and my actions regrettable.

How many times have we spoken in anger, only to regret it the moment the words leave our lips? How many times have we acted out of hurt, inflicting pain on others simply because we didn't know how to process our own? These are the moments when my other self-reminds me to stop, breathe, and realign with the Source.

The Role of the Heart and Mind

The heart is powerful, but it's also unpredictable. It craves immediate gratification, seeking relief from pain at any cost. It doesn't weigh consequences or consider the bigger picture; it simply reacts.

This is why the heart cannot act alone. It needs the guidance of the mind, the wisdom that comes from a connection with God.

The heart and mind, though different in function, are designed to work together.

Like a tablespoon and a teaspoon, each has a unique purpose, and using one in place of the other leads to imbalance. When the heart dominates, chaos ensues.

When the mind rules without heart, life becomes cold and calculated. Harmony lies in their alignment under God's guidance.

The Impact of Emotional Instability

When the heart is unchecked, its instability affects every aspect of life. Emotional chaos takes root, manifesting as anger, frustration, insecurity, and even bitterness. These emotions, left unaddressed, create patterns—cycles of behavior that we repeat over and over again. We pick the same kind of relationships, make the same mistakes, and face the same disappointments, all because we haven't dealt with the root issues.

It's a miserable existence—one that drains our energy, steals our joy, and leaves us feeling stuck.

But my other self knows there's a way out. It whispers truths that I sometimes forget: *You were not created to live in chaos. You were not designed to carry this burden alone. You have access to peace, to clarity, to freedom.*

Reclaiming Control

When my emotions threaten to overwhelm me, my other self steps in, reminding me of the power of choice. I don't have to be a slave to my feelings. I can choose to stop, to think, and to seek God's wisdom before I act. I can choose to let go of the hurt, the anger, and the fear that weigh me down.

This isn't easy. It requires discipline and intentionality. It requires me to confront the parts of myself that I'd rather ignore. But it's necessary. Because when I allow my heart to breathe, when I release the tension and open myself to God's healing, I find strength I didn't know I had.

The heart, when aligned with God, becomes a powerful instrument.

It beats with purpose, drives with passion, and fuels with love. It's no longer a chaotic force but a steady guide, working in harmony with the mind and spirit to fulfill the divine purpose for which I was created.

A Call to Alignment

As I reflect on my other self—the part of me that remains unwavering and connected to the Source—I'm reminded that this is who I'm called to be. It's not an unattainable ideal; it's the reality of walking in alignment with God.

To live as my other self is to live free from fear, rooted in purpose, and guided by faith. It's to recognize that I am not alone, that I have been crafted with care, and that my connection to the Source is unbreakable.

This journey requires effort. It demands that I confront my fears, release my past, and embrace the fullness of who I am in Christ.

But the reward is worth it—a life of peace, joy, and unwavering confidence, knowing that I am bone of His bone, crafted for a divine purpose, and connected to a source that will never fail me.

What makes my other self so compelling is that it exists within me, untouched by the scars of life. It's the version of me that reflects God's original design, unblemished and unwavering. This other self doesn't just represent who I wish to be; it's who I was created to be.

There's a purity, a clarity, and a focus that stands in stark contrast to the confusion and chaos I sometimes feel. My other self is grounded, connected, and resilient—a direct reflection of the Creator's intent.

But the tension remains. How do I bridge the gap between who I am now and this other self? The struggle isn't just external; it's deeply internal.

Fear whispers that I'll never fully live up to this potential.

It tells me that my past mistakes are too great, that the pain I carry is too heavy, that the dreams I hold are too far out of reach. Fear plants seed of doubt, causing me to question not only my abilities but also my worth. The more I allow fear to speak, the more it begins to consume. It builds walls around my heart, convincing me that isolation is safer than vulnerability.

These walls don't just keep others out—they trap me in. They stifle the flow of life, love, and purpose, leaving me stagnant and disconnected. My other self, however, refuses to be caged. It fights against the barriers I've erected, urging me to step out in faith and embrace the fullness of life.

This battle between fear and faith is not just a matter of the heart—it's a matter of the spirit. When fear takes the reins, it clouds my vision and distorts my perspective.

I start to see obstacles instead of opportunities, threats instead of blessings. But when faith rises, it clears the fog, revealing the truth: I am not alone. My other self is never far, and the Source of all strength is always within reach.

One of the greatest lessons I've learned is that my other self-thrives in surrender. When I stop trying to control everything—when I let go of the need to figure it all out and instead trust the process—I begin to experience the freedom and confidence my other self-embodies. This surrender isn't passive; it's active. It requires me to lay down my fears, doubts, and insecurities at the feet of the One who knows me best.

Reconnecting with my other self isn't about achieving perfection; it's about alignment. It's about allowing my heart and mind to operate in harmony, under the guidance of the Spirit.

It's about recognizing that while my emotions are valid, they don't have the final say. It's about choosing faith over fear, time and time again, until it becomes my default response.

In those moments when fear tries to take over, I've learned to pause and remind myself of who I am. Not who I feel like I am in the moment, but who God says I am. I remind myself that I am fearfully and wonderfully made, that I am called for a purpose, and that I am never without hope.

My other self holds tightly to these truths, and when I allow those truths to take root in my heart, I feel the shift. The walls start to come down, the flow begins to return, and the connection to my Source is restored.

This process isn't instantaneous, and it isn't always easy. But with every step, I grow stronger. With every victory, no matter how small, I become more aligned with the person God created me to be.

And with every moment of alignment, I catch a glimpse of the endless possibilities that come with living as my other self.

14

15

Chapter 3: Imbalance

Breakdown occurs when there is an imbalance between the mind and the heart. This imbalance disrupts the harmony needed to stay connected to the Source. The heart and mind must operate in unity, submitting one to the other, to achieve the oneness that brings clarity and peace. One cannot dominate or overpower the other without causing chaos. Their relationship must be an even exchange, a delicate balance, to achieve maximum results.

When the heart rules over the mind, emotions take the lead, pulling you onto an endless roller coaster of highs and lows.

The heart is easily swayed by what it sees, feels, and experiences. It thrives on immediacy, often reacting impulsively to its surroundings.

On the other hand, when the mind leads without the heart's balance, confusion and fear can dominate. The mind, untethered from divine wisdom, becomes a slave to the emotional turbulence that the heart generates.

For balance to occur, the mind must stay connected to the Source. Only then can it walk in guidance, wisdom, and clarity. When the mind is detached from the Source and instead follows the erratic signals of the heart, the path forward becomes difficult to discern. Information flows from the heart to the mind to be processed, but without the steadying influence of the Source, this information becomes distorted. Mixed signals ensue, abruptly shifting focus and direction, leaving a trail of confusion and uncertainty.

The Cost of Imbalance

Imbalance doesn't just affect the way we think or feel—it impacts our ability to

function as a whole. When the heart and mind are out of sync, the bones—the very framework of our existence—cannot remain fitly joined together.

The mind needs time and clarity to process the information it receives from the heart. Rushing this process or allowing one to overpower the other leads to decisions made in haste, confusion, or fear.

The mind, when left unchecked, can be its own worst enemy. It develops ideas and scenarios that play out in dreams, waking moments, and even in the stillness of night. Sleep becomes elusive as the mind runs out of control, conjuring fears, doubts, and imaginary threats. What you give your attention to ultimately controls you. Paranoia sets in, making you distrustful of everything and everyone. You shrink your circle of trust, convinced that only a few can truly understand you or safeguard your vulnerabilities.

This imbalance isolates you, creating a cycle of distance and suspicion. While opposites may attract, enduring relationships are built on commonalities. Without balance, the journey toward unity becomes riddled with friction and resistance. Opposites bring intrigue, but it is the shared values, the harmony between the heart and mind, that create lasting connection and purpose.

Finding Alignment

Our lifelong journey should be to seek out and nurture the commonalities between the heart and the mind. Every part of us must flow in harmony, submitting to the Source to achieve unity.

When one part tries to control or manipulate the other, friction arises. Life becomes a series of three steps forward and five steps back. Progress feels fleeting, and frustration takes hold.

Acknowledging imbalance requires honesty and humility.

It's easy to place blame on external factors or people, but the truth often lies within. Imbalance is born from our own refusal to confront unresolved issues. These issues spill over into our thoughts, emotions, and even our physical well-being. When we ignore them, they grow, creating stress, tension, and disconnection. This disconnection clouds every aspect of life. Expectations drop, self-esteem shatters, identity becomes blurred, and the future seems uncertain. You may project an image of unity to the outside world, but inside, you feel divided—buried under the weight of unresolved conflicts between your heart and mind.

Hope in the Midst of Chaos

But there is hope. No matter how imbalanced life may feel, the moment you recognize the need for change, you've already begun the journey back. Healing and restoration don't happen overnight, but they are possible. The moment you decide to confront the imbalance, the process of reconciliation begins.

Love, joy, and peace await on the other side of the struggle. These aren't just fleeting emotions—they are enduring states of being that come from alignment with the Source. Even in your darkest moments, there are parts of you—stronger, undiscovered parts—cheering you on, urging you to keep going.

You may hear whispers in your soul: *Don't give up. Keep moving forward. It's not over. Failure isn't final. What matters is that you get back up and try again.* These echoes of encouragement remind you that restoration is always within reach.

The mind and heart can find harmony, but only when both submit to the Source. When they align, the tension dissipates, clarity returns, and peace takes root. This isn't just about regaining control; it's about living fully, free from the weight of imbalance.

Imbalance may feel overwhelming, but it isn't permanent. The choice to heal, to reconnect, and to align is always yours.

When you embrace this process, you begin to live in the fullness of who you were created to be—a person of purpose, balance, and divine alignment.

Imbalance doesn't announce itself loudly. Often, it starts as a whisper—an unnoticed shift in the dynamics between the heart and mind. A fleeting thought dismissed, an emotion left unchecked, or a choice made hastily can snowball into a pattern of disconnection. It's only when the weight becomes unbearable that we realize how far we've strayed from alignment.

The beauty, however, lies in the recognition. The moment you acknowledge that something is off, you've taken the first step toward recalibration. Just as a broken bone requires careful resetting to heal, the imbalance between the heart and mind demands intentional effort to restore harmony.

The heart, though volatile, carries the raw material for purpose—dreams, passion, and drive.

Yet without the mind's discernment, those raw materials can be mishandled, leading to impulsive actions and unintended consequences. Similarly, the mind, with its capacity for reason and logic, must lean on the heart's vulnerability to remain compassionate and open. One cannot thrive without the other.

Think of the imbalance as a tug-of-war. When the heart pulls too hard, emotions cloud judgment, making it difficult to see beyond the immediate moment.

When the mind pulls too hard, over analysis paralyzes action, trapping you in a cycle of "what-ifs." The goal isn't for one to overpower the other but for both to work in unison, moving forward together, guided by the Source.

Recognizing the Signs of Imbalance Imbalance reveals itself in subtle yet significant ways. You may feel overwhelmed, as though life is spinning out of control. Sleepless nights, racing thoughts, and constant second-guessing become your norm.

You may find yourself avoiding deep connections with others, fearing judgment or rejection. Or perhaps you notice a pattern of repeating mistakes—choosing the wrong relationships, making impulsive decisions, or staying stuck in fear.

These are not signs of failure; they are opportunities for growth. The imbalance is not an end—it's a signal, a call to realign with the Source. Ignoring it only prolongs the struggle, but addressing it paves the way for healing.

The Importance of Submission

Restoring balance requires submission—not to your circumstances or emotions,

but to the divine guidance of the Source. Submission isn't weakness; it's strength in action.

It's acknowledging that you cannot navigate life's complexities alone. It's recognizing that the heart and mind, though powerful, need direction from something greater.

When the heart and mind submit to the Source, the chaos begins to settle. Clarity replaces confusion. Peace replaces turmoil. Decisions become purposeful, and progress feels steady. This submission isn't a one-time act; it's a daily practice of seeking alignment, listening for wisdom, and allowing the Source to guide your steps.

The Journey Back

Rebuilding balance is a process, and it doesn't happen overnight. It's a journey of small, intentional steps—choosing faith over fear, reflection over reaction, and connection over isolation.

The journey isn't linear; there will be setbacks and challenges. But each step forward, no matter how small, brings you closer to the harmony you seek.

You are not alone in this journey. Even when the imbalance feels overwhelming, know that you are surrounded by unseen support.

The whispers of encouragement you hear—*keep going, don't give up, it's not over*—are not just your own thoughts. They are echoes of divine love, reminders that you are never too far gone to find your way back.

Your heart and mind were designed to work together, each complementing the other's strengths. When they align, you become unstoppable—not because you are perfect, but because you are whole. Balance doesn't mean the absence of challenges; it means the presence of peace in the midst of them.

Every step you take toward balance is a step toward becoming the person you were created to be—a person of purpose, wisdom, and love. Imbalance may have disrupted your path, but it does not define your journey. The process of restoration is underway, and with each passing day, you are moving closer to the harmony you were meant to live in.

16

17

Chapter 4: Road to Recovery

The hope of relief is in sight. Freedom is closer than it feels—only one step away. All you have to do is move. That single, courageous step may seem insignificant in the moment, but it holds the power to shift your entire reality. The path might feel cloudy and dim, but as you move forward, the haze begins to lift, and the way becomes lighter and clearer with every step.

Standing still, you can't see the provisions waiting on the other side. You can't see the opportunities, the blessings, or the healing that has already been activated by your decision to move.

But when you dare to dream one more time, to trust the process and keep the faith, you unlock the possibilities that God has set in motion for you.

The Power of Movement

Movement is essential. It's not just about physical action—it's about shifting your mindset and aligning your heart. When your mind is clear and focused, and your heart is under control, there is nothing that can stop or hold you back. I've come to recognize the crack in my system, the break that has been holding me down and causing my bones to ache.

That recognition is the starting point, the foundation upon which healing is built.

Romans 8:28 reminds us that "all things work together for good to them that love God." This truth fuels my determination to take a leap of faith, to stand firm even when the ground beneath me feels shaky. Recovery begins with a decision—a decision to take control back from fear, doubt, and insecurity, and to place it where it belongs: in the hands of God.

The Risks of Staying Idle

Time moves faster when you're in motion. Doors begin to open, dreams take shape, and what once felt impossible becomes attainable.

But standing still invites danger. Idleness creates space for fear, doubt, and unbelief to creep in. It's in those idle moments that you start talking yourself out of trying, convincing yourself that the obstacles are too great, the journey too long.

Recovery isn't a race. It might take longer for you than it does for others, and that's okay. Every hurt, every pain, every disappointment is different. Your journey is unique, and it cannot be measured by someone else's progress. Comparing your steps to others only leads to frustration. Instead, focus on your own path, understanding that each step forward, no matter how small, is a victory in itself.

Acknowledging the Process

Healing is a process, not an event. My connection wasn't lost overnight.

It took years of suppressed emotions, unmet expectations, and devastating events to bring me to this place.

The recovery process requires patience, grace, and an unwavering commitment to move forward, even when progress feels slow.

Sensitive matters of the heart and the confusion of the mind must be handled with care.

We can't rush to the finish line, hoping to skip over the pain and discomfort. Instead, we must take time to dissect each part of our journey, paying close attention to the details.

Every experience, every hurt, and every moment of brokenness carries a lesson. If we ignore the lessons, we risk repeating the cycles that brought us to this place of imbalance.

Learning to Breathe Again

Recovery isn't about perfection

it's about progress. Give yourself room to breathe and grow. It's okay to stumble—it's part of the journey. The goal isn't to avoid mistakes but to learn from them. Each step forward, no matter how small, is a testament to your strength and resilience.

When you're dealing with years of unresolved pain and suppressed emotions, it can feel overwhelming.

But remember this: you are not beyond repair. The cracks in your system are not the end of your story—they are the beginning of something new. As you move forward, you'll begin to see how even the most painful experiences have shaped you, taught you, and prepared you for what lies ahead.

The Light at the End of the Road

The road to recovery is not easy, but it is worth it. With each step, the weight of the past begins to lift. Love, joy, and peace—the gifts waiting at the finish line—start to feel attainable.

The journey might feel slow, but progress is still progress. Every moment of forward motion, every time you choose faith over fear, is a victory.

Recovery is about reclaiming what was lost—your hope, your identity, your connection to the Source. It's about stepping into the fullness of who you were created to be, knowing that no matter how far you've fallen, the road to restoration is always within reach.

So, move, even when the way seems uncertain. Trust that with each step, the path will become clearer. Dare to believe in the possibilities waiting for you on the other side. The process may be long, but the destination is worth it. As you walk this road, remember: you are not alone, and you are never without hope.

The road to recovery also requires patience—patience with yourself, the process, and the timing of God's plan.

Often, we want results immediately, a quick fix to alleviate the pain or resolve the chaos. But just as a wound takes time to heal, so does the journey to emotional and spiritual wholeness.

Each step you take, even when it feels small or insignificant, is progress.

The cracks in your system are not just weaknesses; they are also openings for light to shine through, revealing areas of growth and strength. When you begin to move, you may notice that clarity doesn't come all at once. At first, it might feel like walking through fog—uncertain, hesitant, and questioning if you're heading in the right direction.

But every step matters. The provisions and possibilities waiting on the other side aren't visible while you stand still. Movement activates faith, and faith opens the door to transformation.

Along this journey, it's important to celebrate progress, no matter how small.

Every time you refuse to give up, every moment you choose hope over despair, is a victory worth recognizing. These small wins remind you that recovery is not just a destination but a process of becoming whole again.

Embracing the Process

It's natural to want to rush to the finish line, to see the fruits of your efforts as quickly as possible. But rushing often leads to overlooking important lessons along the way.

Recovery is not just about reaching a goal; it's about understanding the steps that brought you there. Each layer of pain and disappointment that you peel back holds wisdom. By handling these matters with care, you equip yourself to handle future challenges with grace and resilience. Your journey is uniquely yours. Don't measure your progress against the timeline or achievements of others.

Some wounds take longer to heal because they run deeper. Comparing yourself to others only adds unnecessary weight to your journey. Instead, focus on the strides you've made. Even the act of recognizing the cracks in your system is a significant step forward.

Moving Forward with Faith

As you continue to take steps, the momentum you build will start to shift your perspective. What once felt overwhelming will begin to feel manageable. What seemed like insurmountable pain will become a chapter of growth and strength. Each step forward is a choice to trust God's plan, even when you don't see the full picture.

Faith is what fuels the journey. It's the belief that, despite the setbacks and challenges, something greater awaits you.

Faith doesn't eliminate the hard days, but it gives you the strength to endure them. It keeps you anchored when doubt tries to pull you backward.

The road to recovery is a testament to your resilience, courage, and ability to trust the process. With every step, you are reclaiming your identity, restoring your purpose, and realigning with the Source. Keep moving forward, even when the way feels uncertain. The clarity and freedom you seek are just beyond the horizon.

18

19

Chapter 5: Journey's End

Admitting there is a problem is often the hardest part of the journey, but it's also the beginning of freedom. By confronting the lingering issues, reclaiming control, and uniting the heart and mind, I've laid the groundwork for true healing. Now what? This is where the process shifts. Healing is no longer a hope; it is a reality. Nothing can hold me back because I've realized one of life's greatest truths: what I've been searching for all along was always within me.

The Power of Responsibility

Taking full responsibility for the areas of my life that have been out of place is both humbling and empowering.

It's easy to point fingers, to blame circumstances, people, or past failures.

But when I accepted that the power to heal and move forward rested in me, everything changed. Responsibility isn't about blame—it's about reclaiming your power. It's about acknowledging that while you may not control what happened to you, you can control how you respond and grow from it.

No matter where I've been—whether in valleys of despair or on mountains of triumph—one thing has remained constant: the presence of my Leader, Guide, and Teacher. God's hand was always there, nudging me forward, even when I couldn't see it. The moments of uncertainty, the questions that seemed unanswered, were all tools He used to prepare me for this process of healing.

The Gift of Perspective

Taking a stroll down memory lane isn't always easy, but it's necessary.

Reflection allows me to see the patterns, the lessons, and the moments of growth that I couldn't see while I was in the midst of the struggle. How can I understand what I've gained if I never acknowledge what I've lost? How can I recognize the strength I've built if I don't reflect on the challenges I've overcome?

My past—its challenges, failures, and tears—was not wasted. Every setback was a setup for this moment. It was all preparation. Now that the fog has lifted, I can see things clearly. The experiences that once brought me pain now offer wisdom. The struggles that once felt insurmountable have become stepping stones to a stronger, more fulfilled version of myself.

Letting Go to Move Forward

Walking in bitterness and unforgiveness only weighs us down. Carrying the hurt, resentment, and guilt from the past prevents us from stepping into the freedom God has designed for us.

Releasing myself and others from guilt is not just an act of grace—it's an act of liberation. Forgiveness is not about condoning what happened; it's about choosing not to let it control my present or my future.

Every experience was trying to tell me something was missing in me. I wasn't living fully—I was existing in a cycle of unfulfilled expectations, broken focus, and unrealized potential. But now, with clarity and perspective, I can shift my focus. I no longer look at the past with regret but with gratitude for the lessons it taught me.

Embracing the New

Broken focus yields unripen fruit. I've learned that when my attention is divided—when I'm caught up in pain, doubt, or fear—I cannot bear the fruit I was designed to produce.

But now, my basket is full, and I can embrace the truth that it's okay to focus on myself.

This isn't selfishness; it's stewardship. Nurturing my growth allows me to blossom into the person I was created to be.

It's never too late to start a new chapter. No matter how far I've wandered or how broken I've felt, I am not beyond reconstruction. The rebuilding process is slow, yes, but it's intentional. Day by day, hour by hour, decision by decision—this is how healing unfolds. Each choice I make to forgive, to grow, to believe, and to hope is a step closer to the person I've always dreamed of becoming.

Living in Fullness

As I step into this new chapter, I understand that healing isn't a destination—it's a way of life. It's a commitment to continually learn, grow, and release what no longer serves me. It's about living with an open heart and a clear mind, fully present in each moment.

The journey has been long, and the process hasn't been easy.

But as I stand at this point of realization, I see that every tear, every disappointment, and every moment of uncertainty was worth it. I'm not the same person who began this journey.

I am stronger, wiser, and more in tune with who I was created to be.

This is the end of one journey, but it's also the beginning of something new—a life of fullness, purpose, and alignment. I walk forward with confidence, knowing that the cracks in my system have been mended, and the pieces of my life are coming together beautifully. My past no longer defines me; it equips me. My focus is no longer broken; it is clear. And my heart and mind are no longer at war—they are united, ready to embrace the possibilities ahead.

This journey to healing has taught me one thing above all: I hold the power to choose what my life becomes. Each step of the process—admitting, confronting, and reconciling—has been an act of faith,

a decision to trust that something greater awaits on the other side. And now, standing at the threshold of this new chapter, I am reminded that healing isn't just about mending what's broken; it's about creating something new, something stronger, something full of purpose.

I have discovered that my healing is not just for me. The clarity I now have, the unity between my heart and mind, and the renewed focus I carry are gifts meant to be shared. Every lesson I've learned, every tear I've shed, and every victory I've claimed can serve as a light for others still navigating their journey.

Looking back, I see how fear, doubt, and broken focus once blinded me to the possibilities within me.

But now, I walk with the assurance that no matter how long the road may seem,

each step forward is a testament to God's faithfulness and my willingness to grow. There is no limit to what I can achieve when my heart and mind work in harmony, guided by the Source of all strength.

I no longer fear the unknown. Instead, I embrace it, knowing that the journey ahead is filled with opportunities to grow, serve, and thrive. This is not the end of my story—it's the beginning of a life lived fully and abundantly, free from the chains of the past and anchored in the hope of what's to come.

Healing is not a one-time event—it is a continuous process, a daily decision to embrace growth and alignment with God.

Now that I've faced my fears, mended the cracks, and united my heart and mind,

I can truly begin to live. But healing also comes with responsibility: the responsibility to nurture this newfound balance, to protect it from the influences that once caused chaos, and to share it with others who may still be struggling.

As I look ahead, I am reminded that this journey is more than just personal restoration—it is about living as a reflection of God's love and grace. The clarity and peace

I have found are meant to flow outward, impacting the lives of those around me. This is the beauty of the process: the healing that begins within doesn't stay there. It spreads, creating ripples of hope, inspiration, and transformation.

I now understand that the cracks in my life were not weaknesses but opportunities. They revealed areas where I needed God's touch, areas where His strength could shine through. Every scar tells a story of redemption, and every lesson learned is a tool to navigate the future with confidence and purpose.

As I stand at the threshold of this new chapter, I am filled with gratitude—not just for the healing but for the journey itself. Every step, every tear, every moment of doubt brought me closer to the person I was always meant to be. And now, with a clear mind, an open heart, and an unshakable connection to the Source,

I am ready to walk forward into a life of abundance and fulfillment.

20

Chapter 6: Bone of My Bone

The journey we've taken through this book is one of discovery, healing, and alignment. From recognizing the cracks in our system to uniting the heart and mind, every step has brought us closer to understanding what it truly means to live as *bone of my bone*. But now it's time to bring it all together, to fully grasp how this concept transforms our relationship with ourselves, others, and God.

In Genesis 2:23, Adam declares, "This is now bone of my bone and flesh of my flesh."

While this statement refers to the creation of Eve, it also holds a deeper truth.

It speaks to the unity and oneness we are designed to experience—not just with others but with God. To be *bone of my bone* is to be deeply connected, inseparably linked to the Source of life, strength, and purpose.

This book has been about more than addressing personal struggles or finding healing from past pain. It's been about understanding that our connection to God is the foundation of everything. When we are aligned with Him, the cracks in our system begin to heal, and our lives take on new meaning. The unity between our heart and mind mirrors the unity we are called to have with God—a unity that brings peace, clarity, and purpose.

Living as Bone of His Bone

to truly live as *bone of my bone* is to embrace the truth that we are not alone. God's presence is constant, His guidance unwavering, and His love unconditional. When we live in alignment with Him, we experience the fullness of life He intended for us.

This connection to God doesn't just transform us; it also changes the way we interact with others. As we heal and grow, we become vessels of His love, grace, and wisdom. Our relationships are no longer marked by fear, insecurity, or imbalance but by unity, respect, and mutual support.

Living as **B***one of my Bone* also means recognizing that we are part of something greater. Just as the bones of the body are joined together to form a functioning whole, we are joined with others in the body of Christ. Our healing and growth contribute to the health of the whole, and our individual journeys inspire and strengthen those around us.

A Call to Action

Now that you've journeyed through this book, the question remains: What will you do with what you've learned? Will you take the steps needed to address the cracks in your system? Will you commit to aligning your heart and mind with God?

Will you dare to live as *bone of His bone*, fully connected to the Source and fully present in your purpose?

This book has given you tools, insights, and encouragement, but the next steps are yours to take. Healing is a process, and it requires intentionality. Begin by reflecting on what resonated most with you in these pages. Identify the areas where alignment is needed, and seek God's guidance as you move forward.

Remember, you are not alone on this journey. God walks with you, His Spirit guides you, and His grace empowers you. As you embrace this truth, you will find a deeper connection with Him—a connection that brings freedom, joy, and fulfillment.

Conclusion

Bone of my Bone is not just a concept; it is a way of life. It is a call to live in unity with God, fully aligned with His purpose and fully open to His love.

It is an invitation to embrace healing, growth, and transformation, knowing that the journey is as important as the destination.

As you move forward, carry this truth with you: You were created for connection. With God, with others, and with yourself. Live as *bone of His bone*, and let this connection guide you into the abundant life He has prepared for you.

21

About the Author

Joanna Henton is a passionate writer, speaker, and believer whose words inspire transformation and healing. Drawing from her own life experiences, Joanna has a unique ability to connect with readers on a deep and personal level, offering hope and guidance to those seeking restoration and a closer relationship with God.

A proud mother of two incredible sons, Zachary and Caleb Robinson, Joanna finds joy and purpose in nurturing her family while sharing her journey of faith with others. Her heart for people and her unwavering trust in God shines through in every page she writes.

Joanna's dedication to helping others stems from her belief that every person has the potential to overcome challenges, embrace their purpose, and live abundantly. Through her writing, she aims to remind readers that no matter where they are in life, God's love and grace are always within reach.

When she's not writing or spending time with her family, Joanna enjoys connecting with her community, exploring nature, and discovering new ways to encourage and uplift those around her.

23

www.ingramcontent.com/pod-product-compliance
Lightning Source LLC
LaVergne TN
LVHW041714060526
838201LV00043B/729